EARTH'S CYCLES

The Seasons Cycle

CHERYL JAKAB

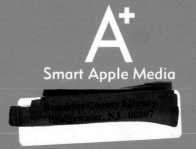

A+

Smart Apple Media

This edition first published in 2008 in the United States of America by Smart Apple Media.
All rights reserved. No part of this book may be reproduced in any form or by any means without written permission from the publisher.

Smart Apple Media
2140 Howard Drive West
North Mankato, Minnesota 56003

First published in 2007 by
MACMILLAN EDUCATION AUSTRALIA PTY LTD
627 Chapel Street, South Yarra, Australia 3141

Visit our Web site at www.macmillan.com.au or go directly to www.macmillanlibrary.com.au

Associated companies and representatives throughout the world.

Copyright © Cheryl Jakab 2007

Library of Congress Cataloging-in-Publication Data

Jakab, Cheryl.
    The seasons cycle / by Cheryl Jakab.
    p. cm. — (Earth's cycles)
    Includes index.
    ISBN 978-1-59920-146-7
    1. Seasons. 2. Earth—Rotation. I. Title.

QB637.2.J35 2007
577.2'3—dc22

2007004552

Edited by Erin Richards
Text and cover design by Christine Deering
Page layout by Christine Deering
Photo research by Jes Senbergs
Illustrations by Ann Likhovetsky, pp. 9, 10, 12, 14, 16, 19, 24; Paul Könye, p. 29.

Printed in U.S.

Acknowledgements
The author and the publisher are grateful to the following for permission to reproduce copyright material:

Front cover photograph: composite of a deciduous tree in four different seasons (center), courtesy of blickwinkel/Alamy; fall leaves (background), courtesy of Corbis.

ARCTIC IMAGES/Alamy, p. 23 (bottom); blickwinkel/Alamy, pp. 1, 22 (bottom); gkphotography/Alamy, p. 7; J Marshall–Tribaleye Images/Alamy, p. 18; Travelshots.com/Alamy, p. 21 (top); Corbis, pp. 4 (middle right & top left), 8, 20 (center & middle right); George McCarthy/CORBIS, p. 6 (both); FCD Photo, p. 22 (top); Laurance B Aiuppy/Getty Images, p. 17 (left); Peter Scholey/Getty Images, p. 25; iStockphoto.com, p. 28 (top); Andrew Davoll/Lochman Transparencies, p. 13 (top); Brett Dennis/Lochman Transparencies, p. 21 (bottom); Jiri Lochman/Lochman Transparencies, p. 17 (right); Dennis Sarson/Lochman Transparencies, pp. 26, 28 (bottom); NASA, pp. 4 (center), 30; Lonely Planet Images/Craig Pershouse, p. 19; Photos.com, p. 15 (bottom); Photodisc, pp. 4 (bottom left, bottom right, middle left & top right), 20 (bottom left, bottom right, middle left & top), 27; Photolibrary.com, p. 23 (top); Lonely Planet Images/Carol Polich, p. 11 (bottom); Jes Senbergs, p. 11 (top); Lonely Planet Images/Dallas Stribley, p. 15 (top); Lonely Planet Images/David Tipling, p. 5; U.S. Fish and Wildlife Service, p. 13 (bottom).

While every care has been taken to trace and acknowledge copyright, the publisher tenders their apologies for any accidental infringement where copyright has proved untraceable. Where the attempt has been unsuccessful, the publisher welcomes information that would redress the situation.

Contents

Summer
Spring
Fall
Winter

ideas and tips

Glossary words
When a word is printed in **bold**, you can look up its meaning in the glossary on page 31.

Earth's natural cycles

What is a cycle?

A cycle is a never-ending series of changes that repeats again and again. Arrows in cycle diagrams show the direction in which the cycle is moving.

Earth's natural cycles create all the environments on Earth. Living and non-living things are constantly changing. Each change is part of a natural cycle. Earth's natural cycles are working all the time.

Earth's non-living cycles are:
- the water cycle
- the rock cycle
- the seasons cycle

Earth's living cycles are:
- the food cycle
- the animal life cycle
- the plant life cycle

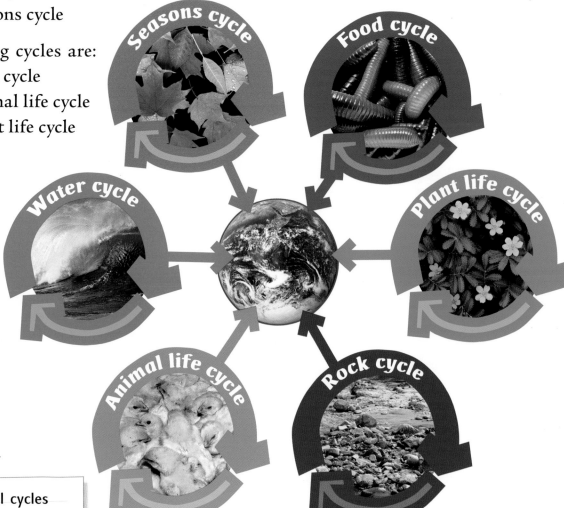

Earth's natural cycles keep the planet healthy.

The balance of nature

Earth's natural cycles all connect with each other. The way the cycles connect is sometimes called the balance of nature.

Keeping the balance

Every living thing depends on Earth's natural cycles to survive. A change in one cycle can affect the whole balance of nature. Knowing how Earth's cycles work helps us keep the environment healthy.

Every living thing depends on the balance of nature to survive.

The seasons

What is a year?

A year is the time it takes for Earth to complete one trip around the sun. The trip takes approximately 365 days. People divide the year into 12 calendar months.

Seasons are times of the year with different kinds of weather. Sometimes the weather is hot, and sometimes it is cold. Each place on Earth has its own pattern of seasons. Most places have four seasons, called summer, fall, winter, and spring. **Tropical areas** have only two seasons, called the wet and the dry. Seasons change from one to the next in a yearly cycle.

Different seasons bring different kinds of weather.

Seasons are important

Seasons are very important to the natural environment. They set the weather patterns in every place on Earth.

Why are seasons important to people?

Seasons affect what people wear and the way they travel. The foods people eat change with the seasons. People heat and cool their homes according to the seasons.

How do people affect seasons?

People are polluting the environment and changing the pattern of the seasons. Pollution is causing **global warming**, which is affecting the weather in every environment on Earth.

How do seasons fit into the balance of nature?

The seasons affect every part of the environment. Animal behavior, food supply, and plant growth can all change with the seasons. Water, rocks, and soil are also affected by the seasons.

In winter, people wear warm clothes when they are outside.

The seasons cycle

The seasons cycle repeats each year. Most places on Earth experience four stages each seasons cycle. They are summer, fall, winter, and spring.

Summer

Fall

Spring

Winter

Seasons change from one to the next in a yearly cycle.

How seasons occur

Seasons occur because Earth's axis is tilted at an angle to the sun. As Earth travels around the sun, different places get more sunlight at different times of the year. This creates the different seasons. When the **Northern Hemisphere** is in summer, the **Southern Hemisphere** is in winter. At the same time of the year, the Northern Hemisphere has the opposite season to the Southern Hemisphere.

What is Earth's axis?

Earth's axis is an imaginary line from the North Pole to the South Pole. Earth spins around on its axis, giving us daytime and night-time. One full spin takes about 24 hours, or one day. The tilt of Earth's axis stays the same all year.

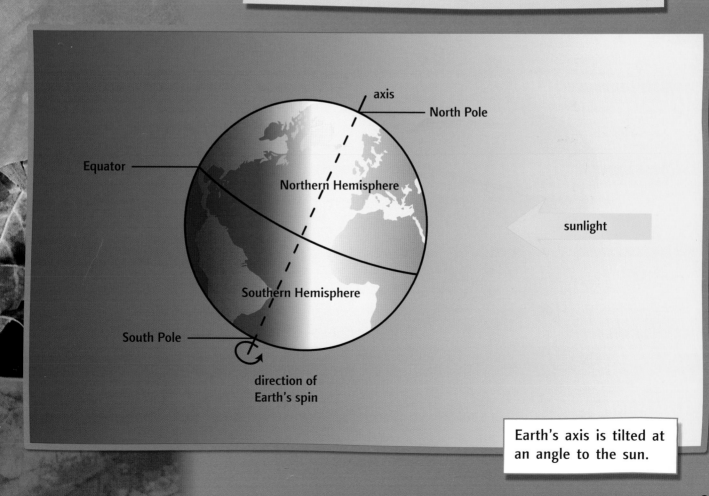

axis

North Pole

Equator

Northern Hemisphere

sunlight

Southern Hemisphere

South Pole

direction of
Earth's spin

Earth's axis is tilted at an angle to the sun.

Summer

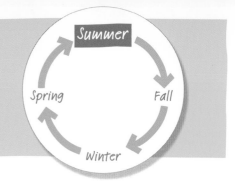

Summer is the season after spring in the seasons cycle. It has the most hours of daylight in each day. Summer is the season with the highest temperatures. The sun is higher in the sky so sunlight falls more directly on Earth. The longest day of the year occurs in summer. It is is called the summer solstice.

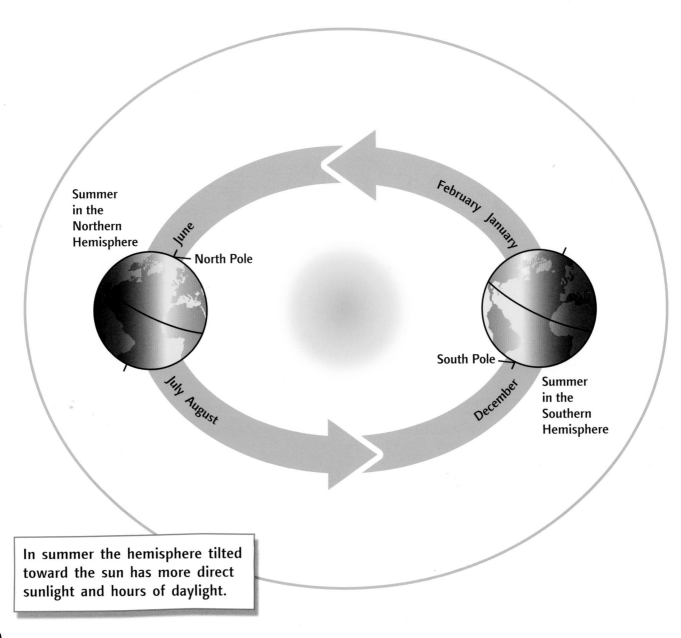

In summer the hemisphere tilted toward the sun has more direct sunlight and hours of daylight.

10

Northern summer

Summer occurs in June, July, and August in the Northern Hemisphere. The weather is hot because the Northern Hemisphere is tilted toward the sun. When the Northern Hemisphere is in summer, the Southern Hemisphere is in winter, because it is tilted away from the sun.

In Alaska, wildflowers come out in summer.

Southern summer

Summer occurs in December, January, and February in the Southern Hemisphere. There are more daylight hours because the Southern Hemisphere is tilted toward the sun. With more hours of direct sunlight, the weather is hot.

In Australia in summer, many people enjoy going to the beach.

11

Fall

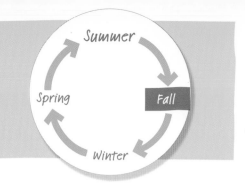

The season that follows summer is fall. The sunlight is not as strong, and the temperatures are cooler. Throughout fall, the days get shorter and the nights get longer. One day in fall has exactly the same amount of daylight and night. It is called the fall equinox.

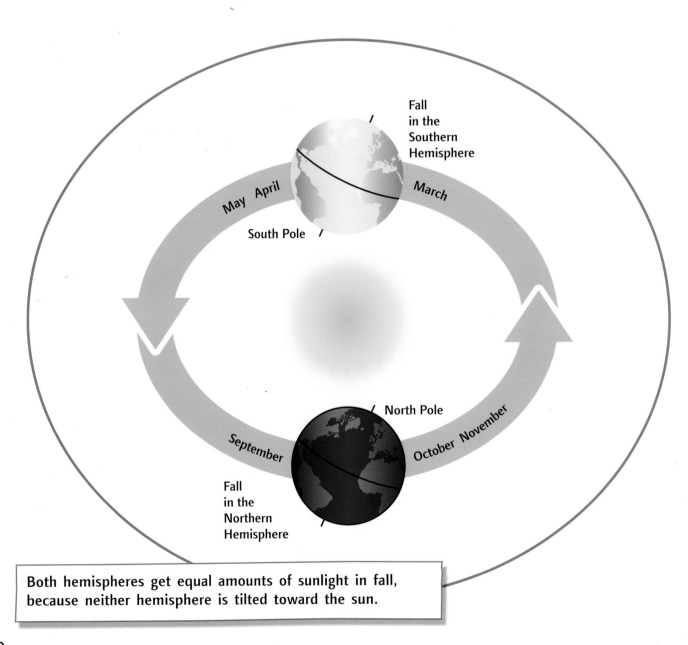

Both hemispheres get equal amounts of sunlight in fall, because neither hemisphere is tilted toward the sun.

Northern fall

Fall occurs in September, October, and November in the Northern Hemisphere. The temperatures get cooler, as the Northern Hemisphere is no longer tilted toward the sun. This season is called fall because many leaves change color and fall from the trees.

The leaves drop from many trees in fall.

Vineyards in the Southern Hemisphere show their beautiful fall colors.

Southern fall

In the Southern Hemisphere, fall occurs in March, April, and May. The hemisphere is no longer tilted toward the sun. Sunlight must travel farther, and is not as intense as in summer. As the days get shorter, there are less hours of sunlight. The extra heat built up over summer is lost.

Winter

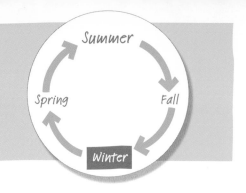

Winter is the season after fall in the seasons cycle. It is the coldest season in the cycle. The sun appears low in the sky, and sunlight is weak. There are fewer hours of daylight and more hours of night. The shortest day of the year occurs in winter. It is called the winter solstice.

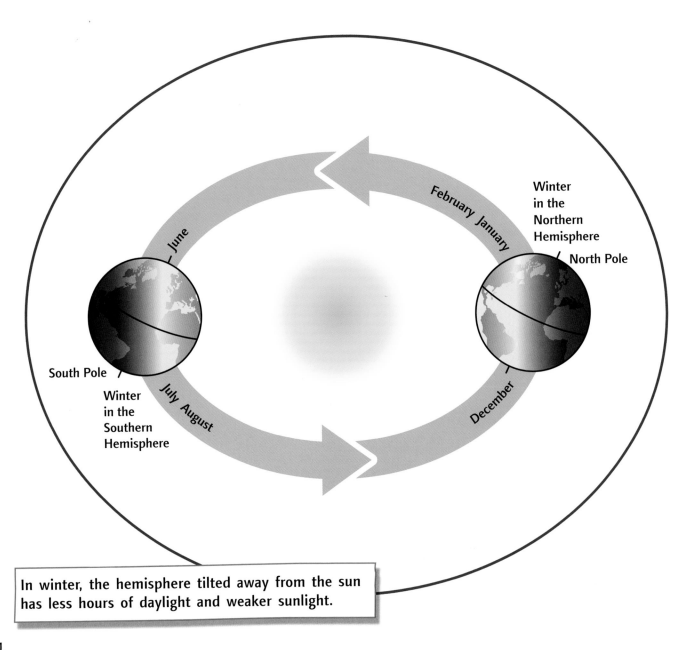

February January

June

Winter in the Northern Hemisphere

North Pole

South Pole

Winter in the Southern Hemisphere

July August

December

In winter, the hemisphere tilted away from the sun has less hours of daylight and weaker sunlight.

Northern winter

Winter occurs in December, January, and February in the Northern Hemisphere. The weather is cold because the Northern Hemisphere is tilted away from the sun. Snow falls in many places during winter. Many trees are bare and plants stop growing. Water in rivers and lakes can freeze into ice.

Southern winter

Winter occurs in June, July, and August in the Southern Hemisphere. The weather is cold and the days are short. There are the fewest hours of daylight, since the hemisphere is tilted away from the sun. During daylight hours, sunlight is weak and spread out. It must travel farther, at an angle through the **atmosphere**, to reach the Southern Hemisphere in winter.

In the Northern Hemisphere, many people enjoy skating on frozen rivers in winter.

Spring

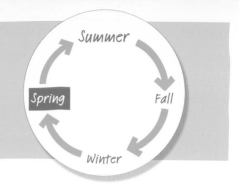

Spring is the season after winter in the seasons cycle. In spring, neither hemisphere is tilted away from the sun. The sunlight is stronger and temperatures are warmer. Spring is the season of increasing daylight hours. Days and nights are more equal in length than in winter or summer. One day in spring has exactly the same amount of daylight and night. It is called the spring equinox.

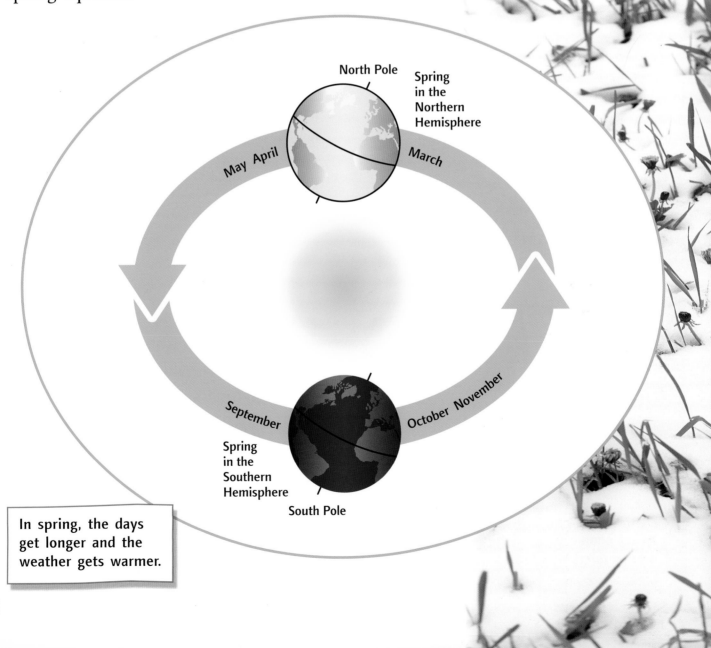

North Pole

Spring in the Northern Hemisphere

May April

March

September

October November

Spring in the Southern Hemisphere

South Pole

In spring, the days get longer and the weather gets warmer.

16

Northern spring

Spring occurs in March, April, and May in the Northern Hemisphere. Temperatures are warmer because the Northern Hemisphere no longer tilts away from the sun. The sunlight warms the ground and snow and ice begin to melt. Plants start growing again and many trees sprout new leaves.

Wildflowers come out in the spring.

As ice melts in spring, new plants begin to grow.

Southern spring

Spring occurs in September, October, and November in the Southern Hemisphere. As Earth continues its **orbit**, the Southern Hemisphere no longer tilts away from the sun. Temperatures are warmer because there is more sunlight, and more hours of daylight. The spring equinox in the Southern Hemisphere is around September 21.

17

Tropical and polar seasons

What is the Equator?

The Equator is an imaginary line around Earth's middle. It separates the Northern and Southern hemispheres. As Earth orbits the sun, sunlight shines directly at the Equator all year round.

Seasons in tropical areas

Tropical areas are areas near the Equator. The sun shines directly through the atmosphere at the Equator, making tropical areas hot all year round. Tropical areas have only two seasons each year. These are called the wet and the dry. The wet is hot and sticky, with lots of rain. The dry is also hot, but does not have as much rain. In tropical areas, days and nights are about 12 hours each throughout the year.

Even in the wet season, the weather is still warm in tropical areas.

Seasons at the poles

At the North Pole and South Pole, the seasons are always cold. sunlight reaches the poles at an angle, making it very weak. The tilt of Earth's axis makes summer at the poles one long day, and winter one long night. For the six months of summer, the sun is always in the sky. In winter, the sun does not rise at all. For six months it is dark and very cold.

At the South Pole in summer, the sun gets low in the sky but never quite sets.

axis

North Pole

Equator

day

night

sunlight

South Pole

direction of Earth's spin

atmosphere

For six months of each year, one pole has constant daylight and the other has night.

The balance of nature

The balance of nature shows how the seasons cycle is linked with Earth's other cycles. The seasons have an effect on non-living and living things in every environment on Earth. The cycles of water, rock, food, plant life, and animal life are all affected by the seasons.

Food cycle

Animal life cycle

Plant life cycle

Seasons cycle

Water cycle

Rock cycle

The seasons cycle is an important part of the balance of nature.

Seasons, rocks, and soil

Seasons have a big effect on rocks and soil. Repeated cycles of heating and cooling can break even the biggest rocks apart. In spring after heavy rain or when ice and snow melt, fast-flowing rivers can cut through the land. The rivers carry rocks and soil along, and deposit them when they slow down.

In spring when the snow melts, rushing rivers carry along rocks and soil.

Seasons and water

Seasons help water move through the water cycle. The amount of water in the air changes with the seasons. When it is hot, more water **evaporates** into the air. Water vapor in the air forms clouds, and falls back to Earth as rain.

Rain clouds are filled with many tiny droplets of water.

Seasons and animals

Animal behavior can change with the seasons. Some animals, such as bats, **hibernate** during winter. Birds often **migrate** to new areas in fall. Many animals reproduce in spring and summer.

Birds often migrate to new places in fall, looking for food.

Seasons and plants

Many plants, such as **deciduous trees**, grow according to the seasons cycle. Deciduous trees grow more quickly in spring and summer. Their fruits ripen in fall and they drop their leaves. Growing slows down in winter, and new leaves appear in spring.

spring

summer

winter

fall

A deciduous tree has bare branches in winter.

Seasons and food

Food availability changes with the seasons. There is normally more food for animals in spring, summer, and fall. Winter in most places is a time when food is hard to find. In tropical areas, the seasons do not change as much. Animals can usually find food throughout the year in these areas.

Squirrels gather nuts in fall to eat in winter, when food is hard to find.

Seasons and food for people

People grow most of their food according to the seasons. This means certain foods are only available in the growing season. However, modern farming methods and technologies, such as greenhouses and **irrigation**, mean that many foods can be grown all year round.

A greenhouse creates the growing conditions that normally happen only in spring.

People and seasons

People's activities can have an effect on the natural cycle of the seasons. This normally happens over a long period of time. Pollution from burning coal and oil is increasing the greenhouse effect in Earth's atmosphere. This is causing global warming. Global warming is changing the pattern of the seasons.

The greenhouse effect

Greenhouse gases are a natural part of the atmosphere. They trap some of the heat from the sun, while the rest escapes back out to space. The trapped heat in the atmosphere warms Earth's surface. This is called the greenhouse effect and it is the natural warming of Earth.

sunlight

escaping heat

trapped heat

greenhouse gases

atmosphere

Greenhouse gases trap heat in Earth's atmosphere.

Global warming

Today there is an increase in the greenhouse effect, which is causing global warming. As people burn coal and oil for electricity and in cars, extra greenhouse gases are released into the atmosphere. The extra gases trap more heat in the atmosphere and increase the warming of Earth.

The average temperature on Earth has risen by more than one degree in the past 60 years. This rise in temperature is changing the weather. Summers are hotter and winters are colder. There are also bigger storms, such as hurricanes, and more of them.

Some power plants burn coal to make electricity, releasing greenhouse gases into the atmosphere.

Preventing global warming

Global warming threatens the balance of nature. The fight to prevent it is a worldwide problem. Using alternative energy and planting more trees are two ways people can help prevent global warming.

Alternative energy

Using alternative energy can reduce the amount of greenhouse gases in the atmosphere. Many alternative energies are being explored. Wind energy and solar power are two alternatives that could replace burning coal and oil in the future.

More trees

Planting trees and not cutting down forests can help stop global warming. Trees absorb **carbon dioxide**, which is a major greenhouse gas. More trees on Earth would absorb more carbon dioxide and reduce the amount of greenhouse gases in the atmosphere.

Planting more trees will help reduce the amount of greenhouse gases in the atmosphere.

The Kyoto Protocol

The Kyoto Protocol was the first set of goals developed to fight global warming. It was developed by the **United Nations** at a meeting in Kyoto, Japan in 1997. Countries were asked to reduce the amount of greenhouse gases they produce by a certain date. More than 160 countries have signed the agreement. The United States and Australia are two countries that have not signed the Kyoto Protocol.

Some countries use solar power to reduce the amount of greenhouse gases they produce.

Reducing greenhouse gases

Everyone can help try to lower the amount of greenhouse gases in the atmosphere. Reducing energy use and recycling can help slow down global warming.

Reduce energy use

- ⟳ Switch off lights when you leave a room
- ⟳ Walk or ride a bike instead of using a car
- ⟳ Switch off appliances at the wall when you do not need them

Riding a bike is better for the environment than traveling by car.

Recycle

- ⟳ Recycle paper to reduce the need to cut down trees
- ⟳ Recycle glass, metals, and plastic to reduce the need to use raw materials

Aluminum cans can be recycled into new cans.

Plant a tree

Trees absorb carbon dioxide, a major greenhouse gas. Help fight global warming by planting a tree or organizing a tree planting project in your area.

What you need

- a young tree
- shovel
- watering can filled with water
- planting site—get permission before you start!

What to do

1 Dig a hole at the planting site. Make it as deep as the roots of your tree and twice as wide.

2 Remove the tree from its container. Carefully place the tree inside the hole.

3 Pack soil around the roots of the tree. Fill the hole with soil, making sure the roots are completely covered.

4 Finally, use your watering can to water the tree. This will help the tree settle into its new home.

Water your tree every week unless it rains.

Living with nature

We all depend on the balance of nature for our survival. If people continue to disturb Earth's cycles, it will upset the balance of nature. Understanding Earth's cycles helps us care for Earth and live in harmony with nature.

"The Earth does not belong to us: we belong to the Earth."

(Chief Seattle Suquamish leader, about 1854)

Glossary

atmosphere	layer of gases surrounding Earth
carbon dioxide	gas that plants take from the air as they live and grow
deciduous trees	trees that lose their leaves once a year
evaporates	when liquid turns into gas
global warming	extra warming of Earth due to extra greenhouse gases in the atmosphere
greenhouse gases	gases that keep heat trapped in the atmosphere
hibernate	sleep through winter to save energy
irrigation	method of watering large areas of farmland
migrate	move from one area to another
Northern Hemisphere	one half of Earth, from the North Pole to the equator
orbit	the path a planet takes around the sun
Southern Hemisphere	one half of Earth, from the South Pole to the equator
tropical areas	warm areas near the Equator (the imaginary line around Earth's middle)
United Nations	group of countries that work together to promote peace and cooperation

Index